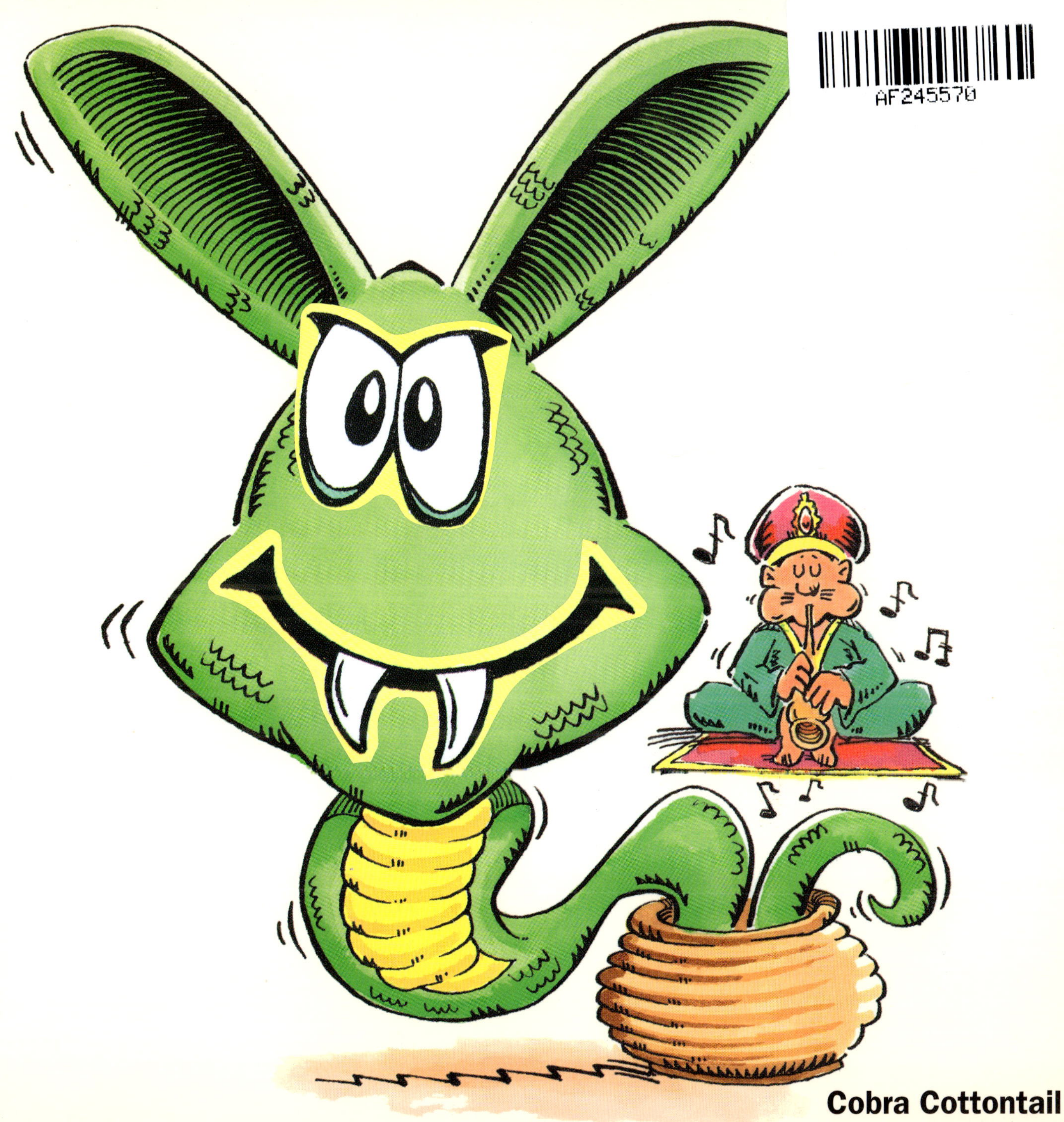

Cobra Cottontail

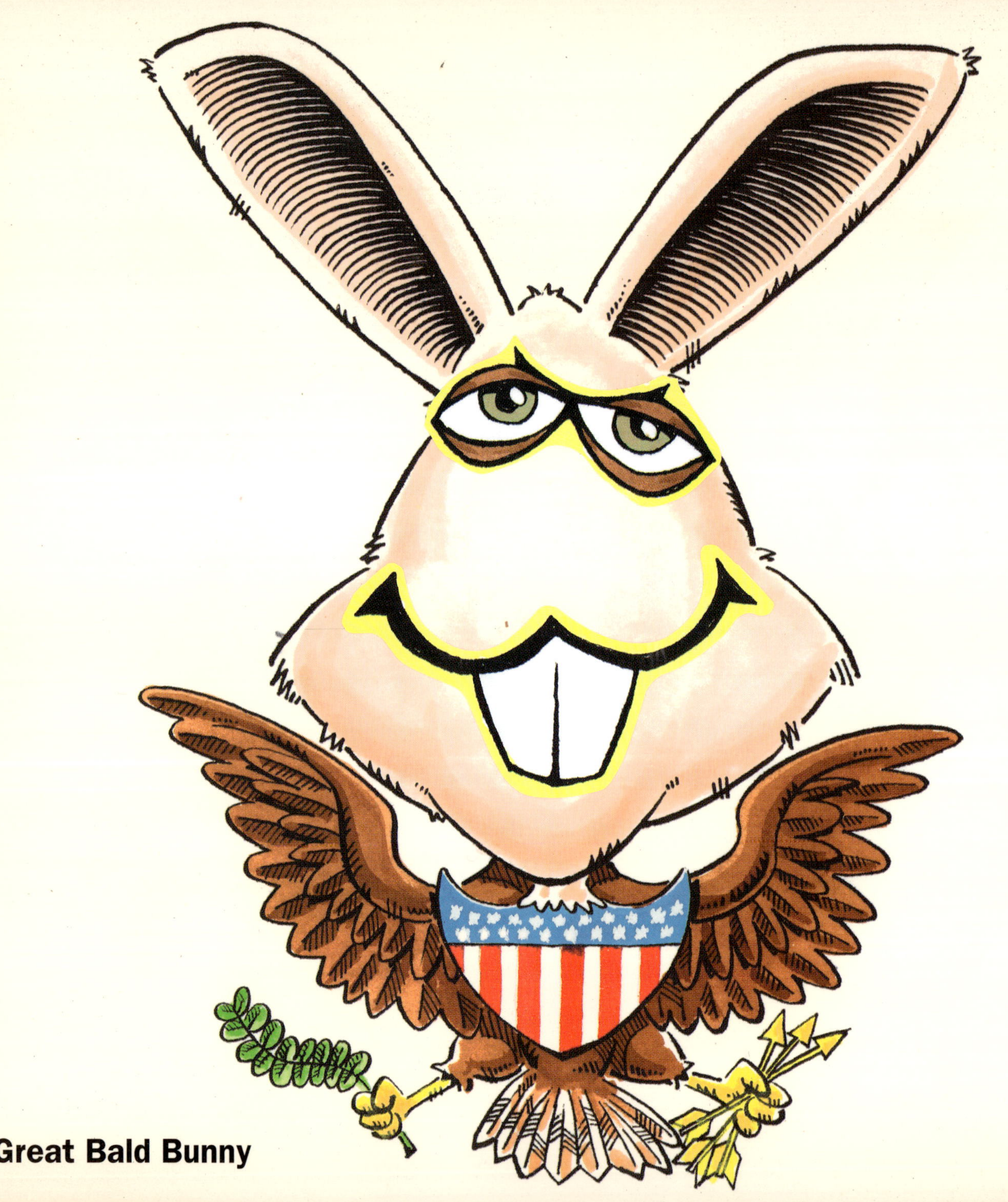

Great Bald Bunny

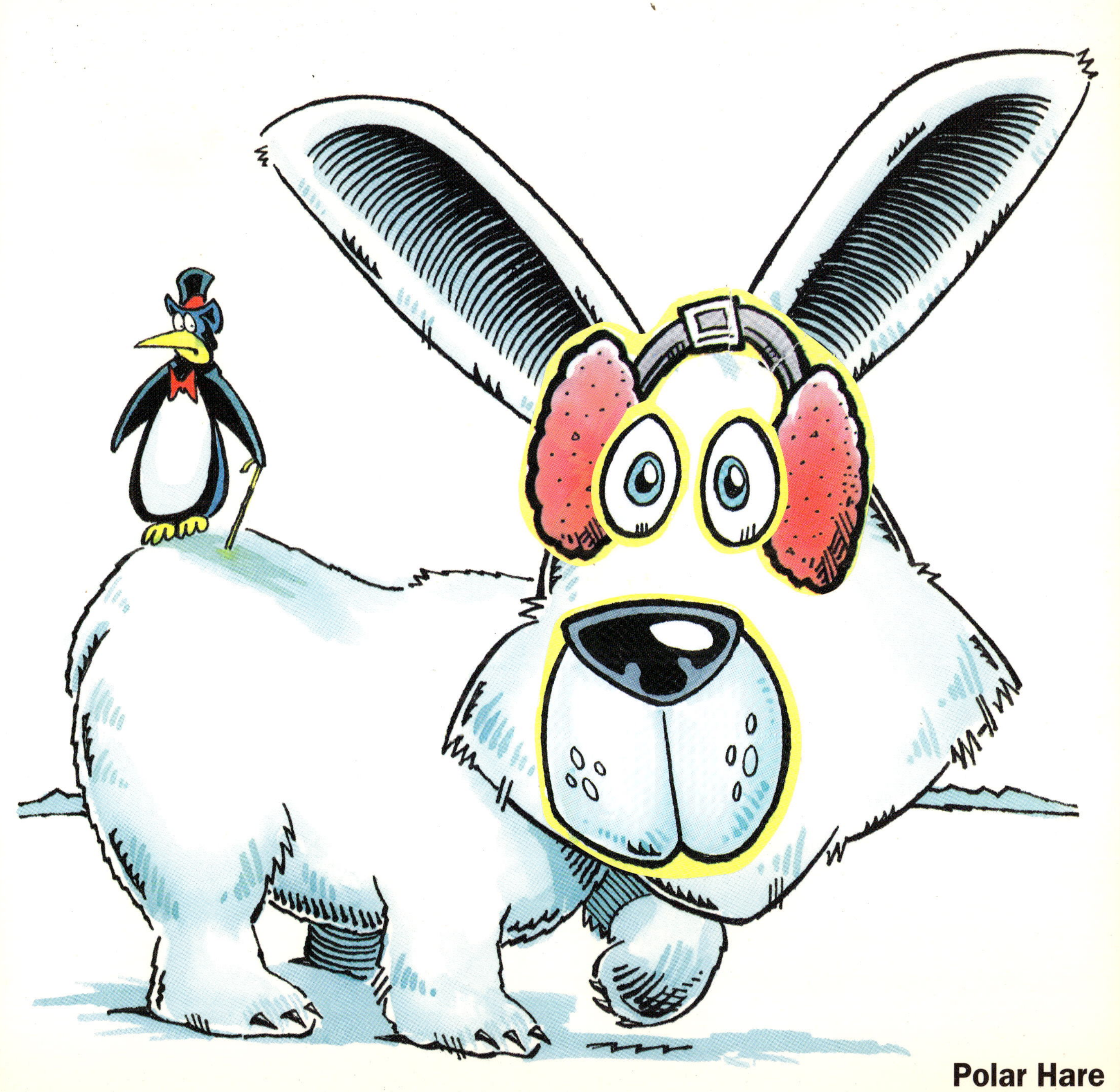

Polar Hare

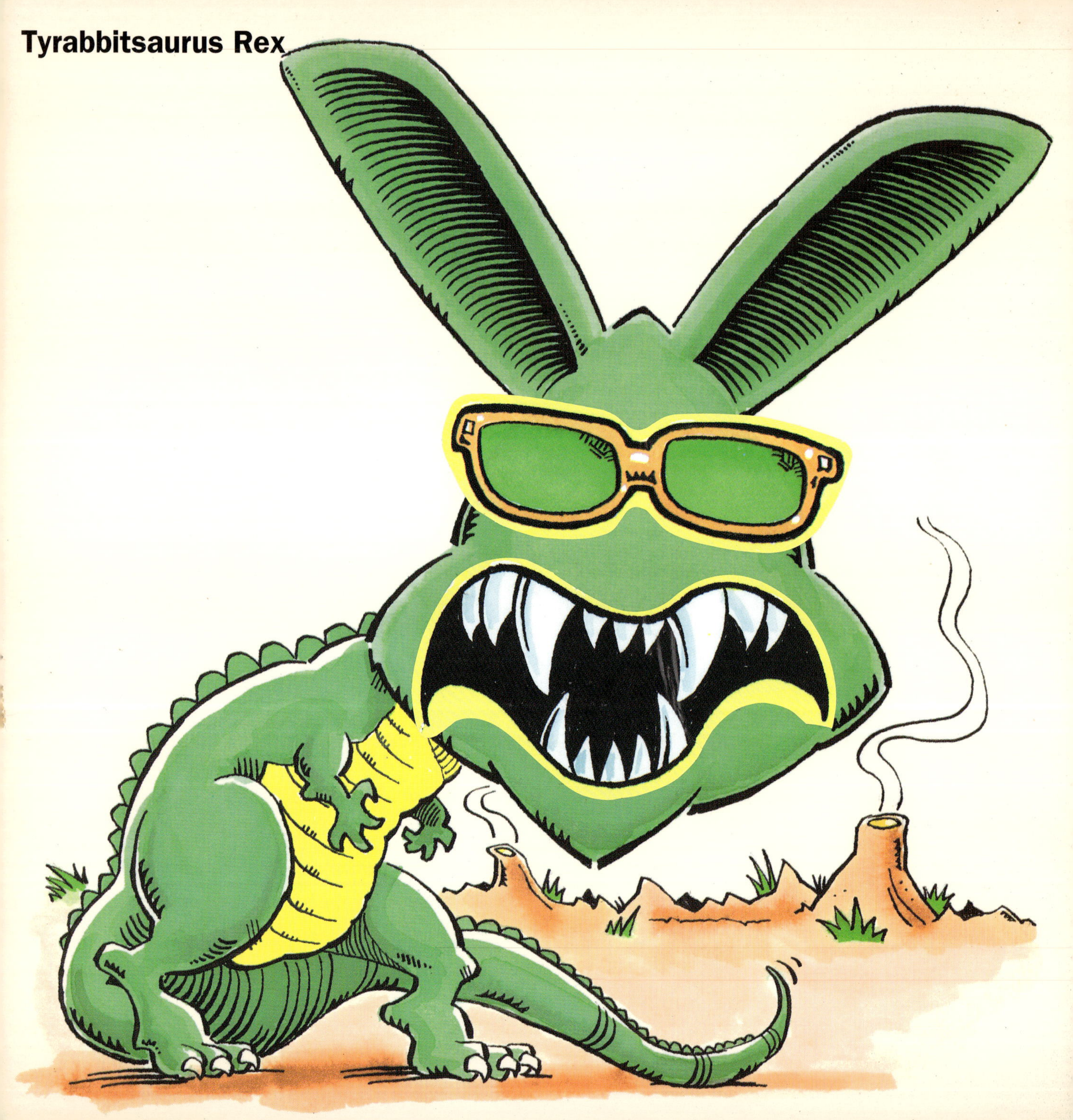

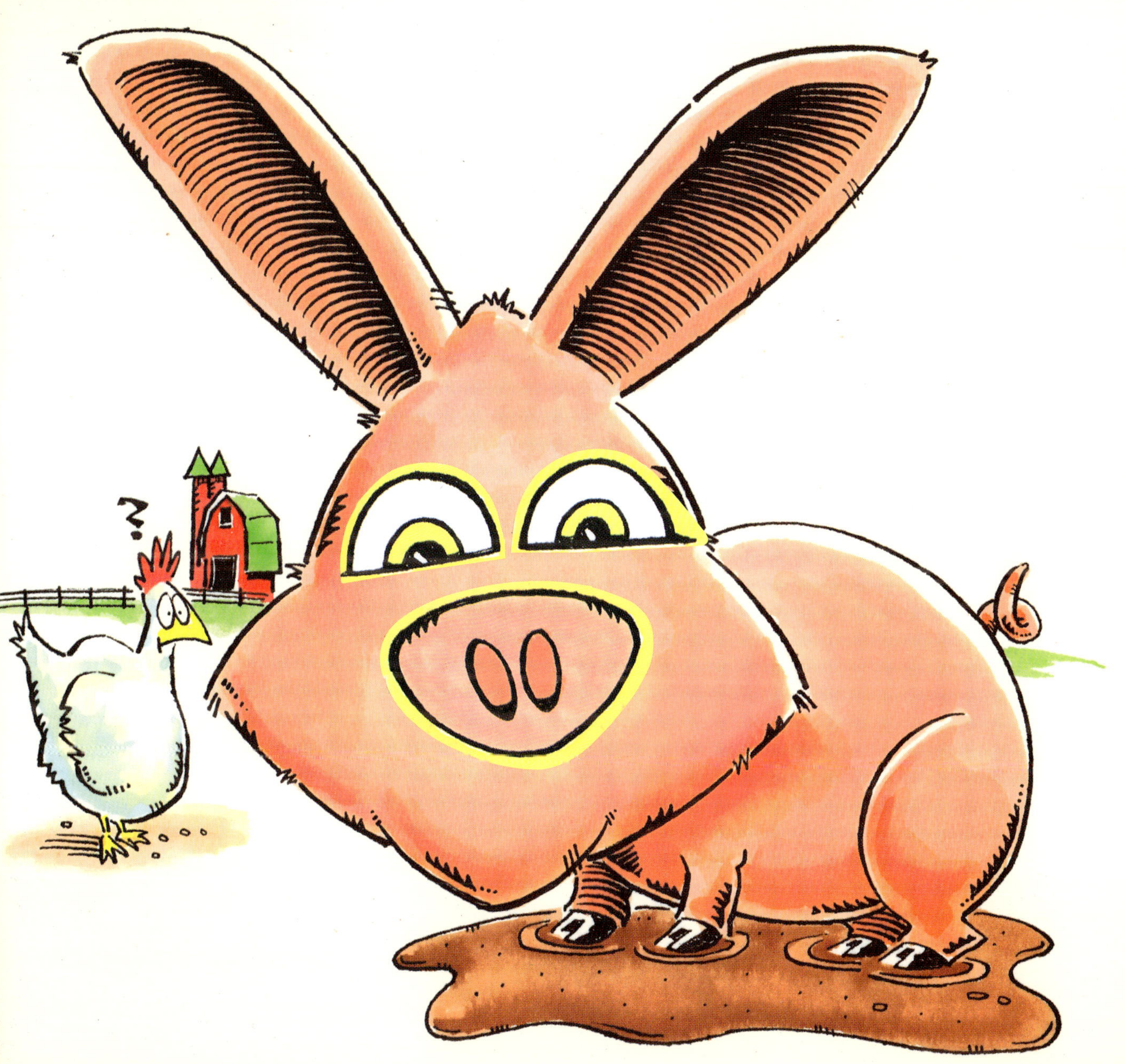

Hopp N. Hogg

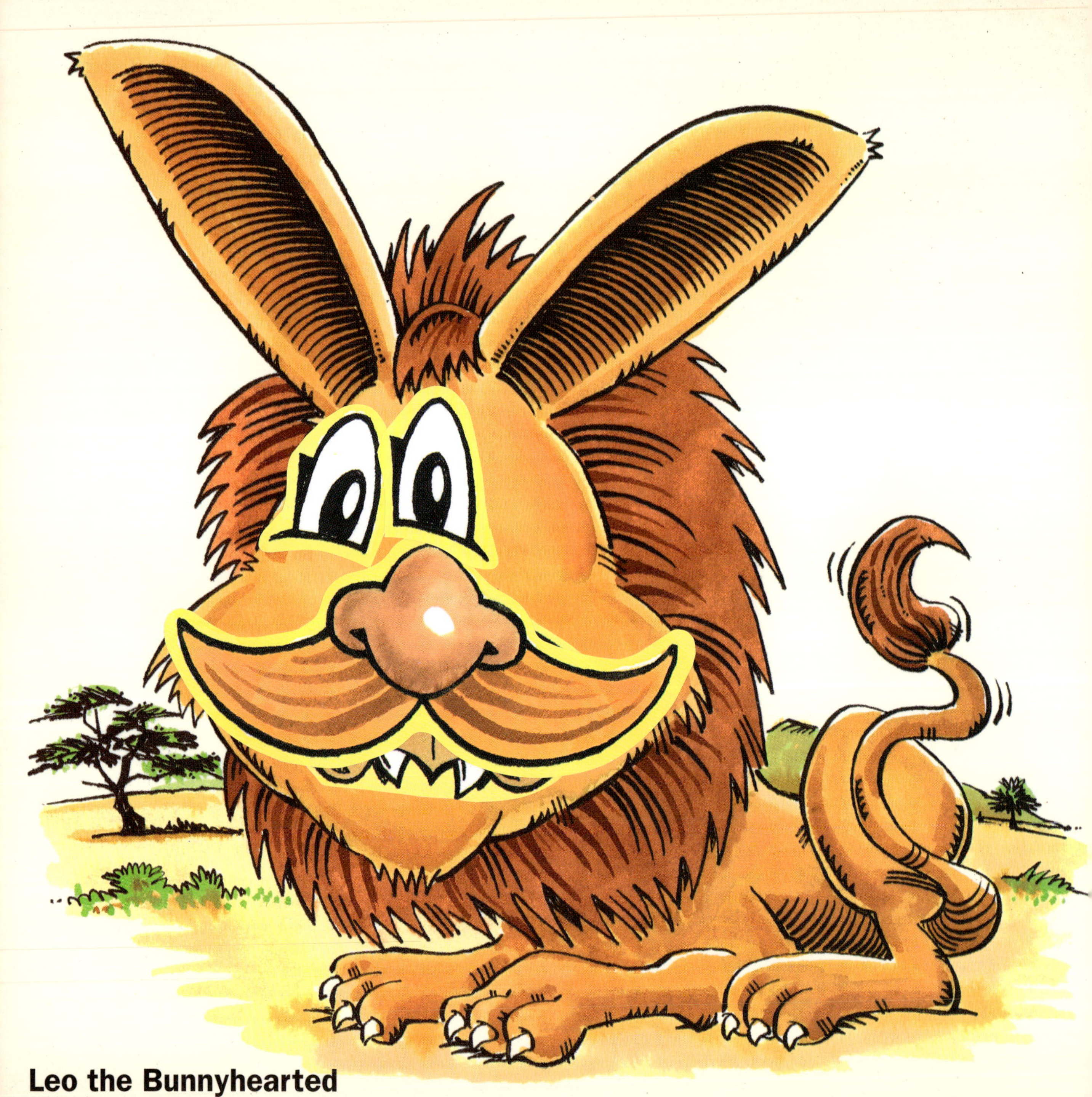

Leo the Bunnyhearted

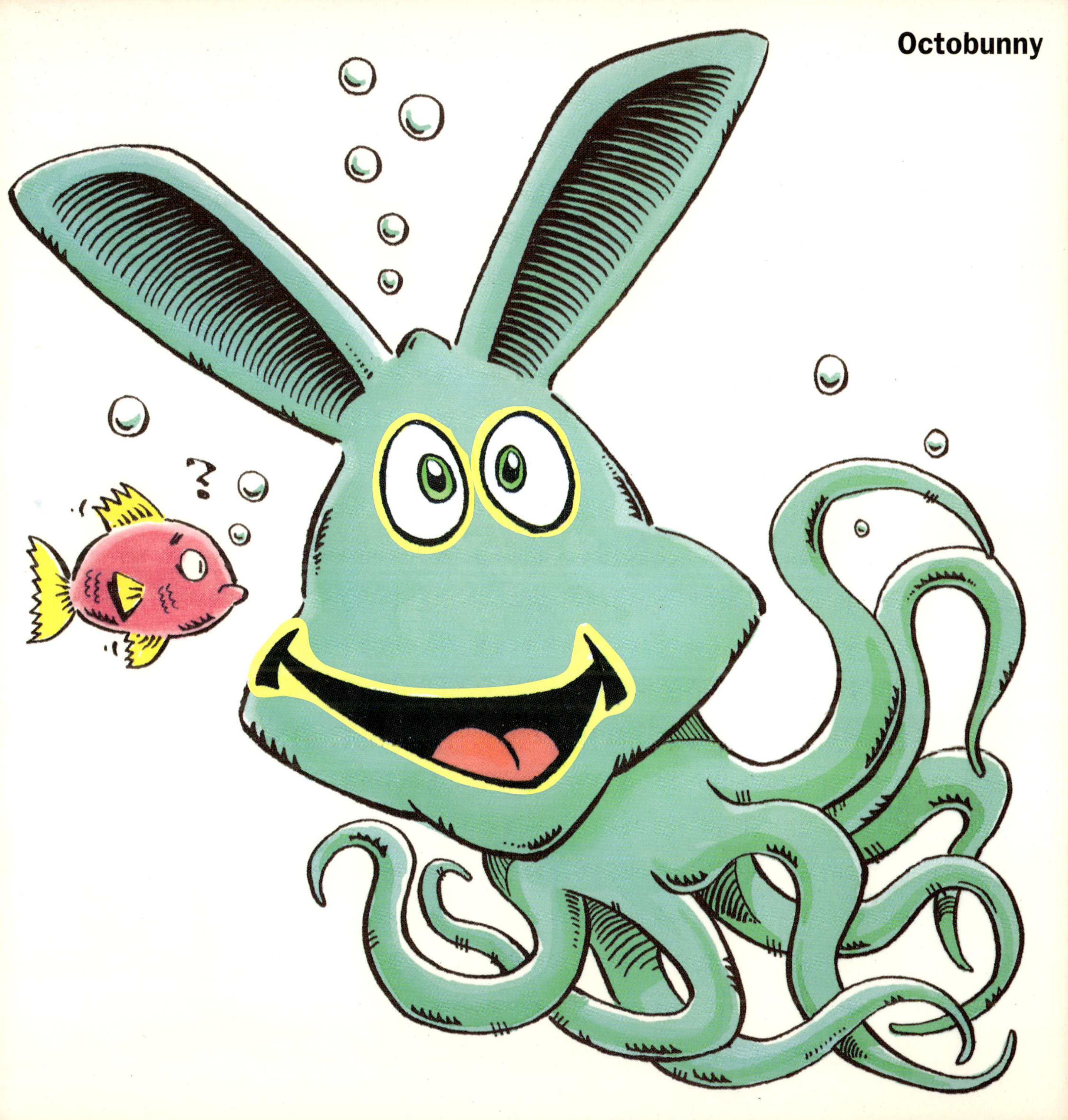

Bunn E. Phant

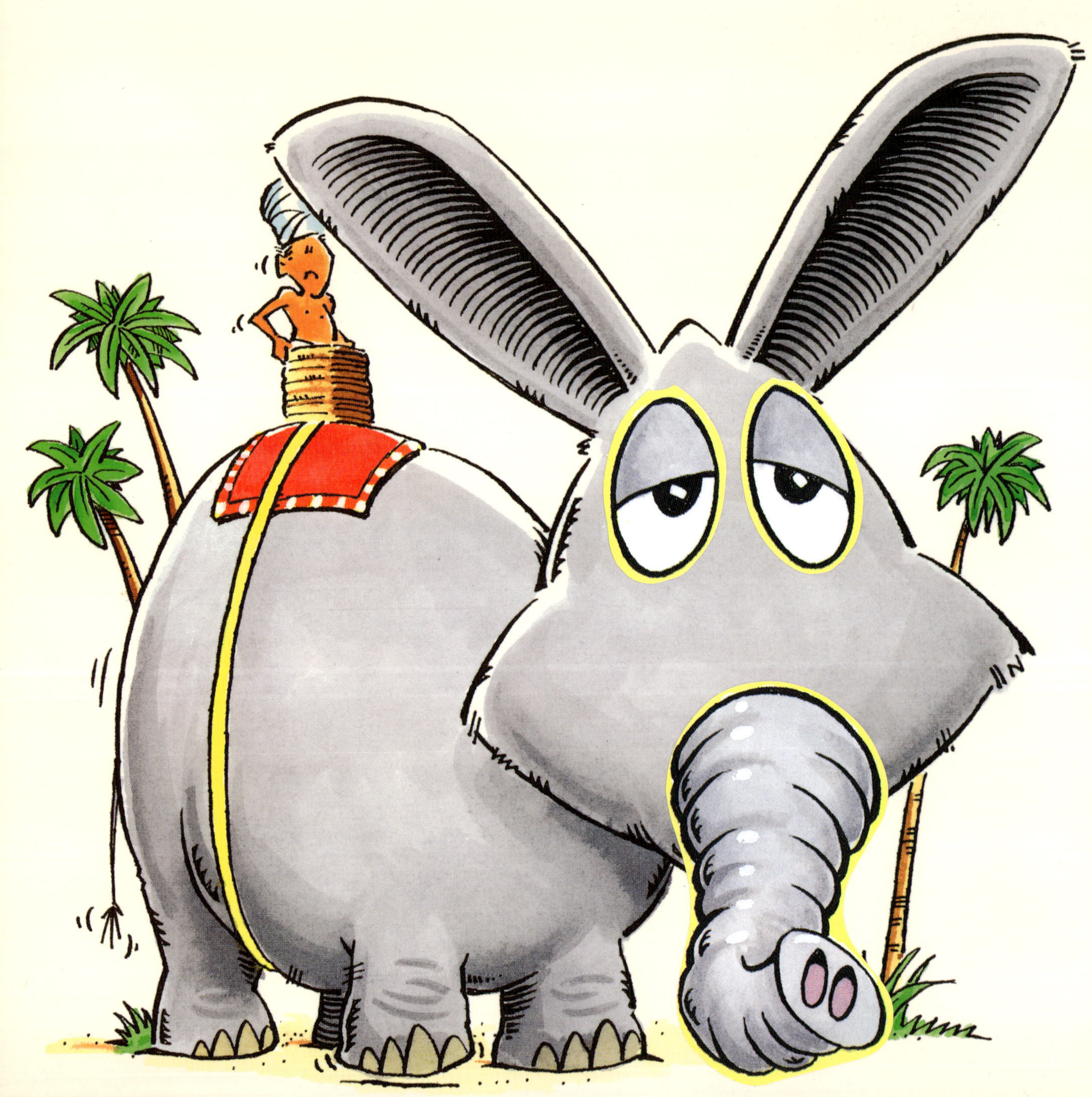